BIG BU$INE$$

Cadbury

Cath Senker

First published in 2012 by Wayland

Copyright © Wayland 2012

Wayland
338 Euston Road
London NW1 3BH

Wayland Australia
Level 17/207 Kent Street
Sydney, NSW 2000

Managing editor: Debbie Foy
Designer: Emma Randall
Picture researcher: Shelley Noronha

Picture Acknowledgments: The author and publisher would like to thank the following for allowing their pictures to be reproduced in this publication: cover image: David J Green/Alamy; 1 iStock; 4 Leslie Garland Picture Library/Alamy; 5, 6, 7, 8, 9, 10, 12, 13B Kraft Foods UK; 11 ©Picture Alliance/Photoshot; 13, 14, 22 ©Photoshot; 16 News (UK) Ltd/Rex Features; 17 Mary Evans / Retrograph Collection; 18 Cadbury World, Dunedin N.Z; 19 Darren Staples/Reuters/Corbis; 20 India Today Group/Getty Images; 21 ©UPPA/Photoshot; 23 Rex Features; 24 Eye Ubiquitous/Photoshot; 25 Getty Images; 26 Facundo Arizabalaga/Rex Features; 27 iStock. Every attempt has been made to clear copyright for this edition. Should there be any inadvertent omission please apply to the publisher for rectification.

British Library Cataloguing in Publication Data
Senker, Cath.
Cadbury : the story behind the iconic business. -- (Big business)
1. Cadbury Ltd.--Juvenile literature. 2. Confectioners--
Great Britain--Juvenile literature. 3. Chocolate
industry--Great Britain--Juvenile literature.
I. Title II. Series III. Senker, Cath.
338.7'6413374'0941-dc23

ISBN: 978 0 7502 6923 0

Printed in China
Wayland is a division of Hachette Children's Books, an Hachette UK company.
www.hachette.co.uk

Contents

Sweet success

Most people are familiar with the sweet, creamy taste of Cadbury's chocolate. Cadbury is a global confectionery company with factories across the world, from Europe to Africa, America, Asia and Australia. It is the market leader in chocolate confectionery in India, and its Dairy Milk is a leading brand worldwide.

Cadbury creates a wide range of products. Go into any newsagent's shop and you'll see a display of Dairy Milk, Bournville, Fudge, Flakes and Crunchies – snacks that have been favourites for decades. As well as chocolate bars, the company makes boxes, bags and tins of confectionery. It produces chocolate cakes and biscuits, ice cream and desserts – not forgetting drinking chocolate and cocoa.

Cadbury was founded in England in the early 19th century as a family company. The profits were ploughed back into the business, workers were offered many benefits, and the company donated money for community projects.

▼ *A range of popular Cadbury chocolate bars on display in a newsagent's shop.*

Chocolate eggs rolls off the Cadbury assembly line ready for wrapping.

Business Matters

The Cadbury business model

By 2000, Cadbury owned factories across the world. It had a franchise agreement with US chocolate company Hershey, which allowed Hershey to make and distribute Cadbury products in the USA. It also had many subsidiary companies making its chocolates — Cadbury owned the majority of shares in these companies and so controlled them. In 2010 Cadbury itself became a subsidiary of Kraft Foods.

In 1962, Cadbury became a public company and the general public could then invest in it. In 2010, the US-based multinational company Kraft Foods took over Cadbury, and it was no longer an independent business.

This book tells the story of Cadbury, one of the main movers and shakers in the confectionery world that helped to transform a little-known drink consumed by the rich into a range of highly popular, affordable treats. It highlights the key figures who took risks to shape Cadbury's development according to their principles, and charts the influence of the Cadbury business on the wider community.

> These days there are thousands of types of chocolate to choose from – you can drink it, eat it, spread it on a sandwich, pour it on your ice cream or make cocktails with it. There's also a growing interest in organic cocoa and [the] wellbeing ... of cocoa farmers around the world.
>
> *Cadbury website, 2012*

The founder: John Cadbury

Cadbury's founder was a Quaker named John Cadbury. Although Christians, the Quakers were not members of the Church of England and they suffered discrimination. They were not allowed to go to university or to enter the professions, for example, to become lawyers or doctors.

In the late 18th and 19th centuries, some Quaker families decided to enter the confectionery business. Quakers believed in improving society. They felt that drinking alcohol was wrong and were keen to provide less healthy treats for people to enjoy.
As well as the Cadburys, the Frys of Bristol and the Rowntrees and Terrys of York became confectioners.

John Cadbury first opened his grocer's shop in Birmingham in 1824, selling cocoa powder to make drinks. He made it by roasting cocoa beans, and pressing and pounding them into a powder. John prepared the cocoa powder himself with a pestle and mortar. The powder was then formed into a cocoa cake to be sold. The consumers scraped off a little to mix with water or milk for drinking.

▼ *An early shop selling chocolate treats – made by Cadbury and Frys.*

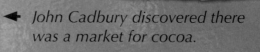
Brains Behind The Brand

John Cadbury – marketing
From the start, John was extremely talented at promoting his business. His shop had an expensive plate-glass window for people to peer in, and he employed a Chinese man, wearing full national costume, to serve in the shop. This drew attention to the business. John's first newspaper advert stated, 'John Cadbury is desirous of introducing to particular notice "Cocoa Nibs", prepared by himself, an article affording a most nutritious beverage for breakfast.' This was seen as a snappy advert at the time!

Business Matters

Transport — A factory had to be located close to transport links, which in the early 19th century meant near a river or canal so that boats could shift the goods. In 1847 Cadbury moved to a new factory in Bridge Street. The site had a private canal spur (short canal) to connect the factory to the Birmingham Navigation Canal, which had links to all the major ports in Britain.

In 1831 John started manufacturing cocoa powder on a larger scale. He rented a small factory in Birmingham and installed a steam engine – a great novelty at the time – for roasting and pressing the beans. By 1842, John was selling 16 types of drinking chocolate and 11 cocoas. Yet the cocoa in his products was not pure. Cocoa beans contain a lot of fat. Confectioners at the time were unable to remove it, so they added starches such as potato flour to make the product easier to digest.

In 1847 John Cadbury formed a partnership with his brother Benjamin and changed the company name to Cadbury Brothers. During this decade, they started to make eating chocolate too. Would this exciting new venture succeed?

The Cadbury business went downhill in the 1850s, mainly as a result of bad luck. First, John's wife died in 1855, then he himself became ill. He ended the partnership with his brother, and in 1861, John's sons George and Richard took over the company.

George and Richard, just 25 and 21 years old, invested all the money their mother had left to them in Cadbury. They were taking a big risk. If they couldn't turn the business round, they would have to close the factory. There was no question of going into debt; the Quaker community would not tolerate it. The pair cut out all luxuries from their lives and devoted themselves to sheer hard work. For the first five years, they put in long hours for a small income.

In the early 1860s, the business was still not thriving, and Cadbury faced severe competition from other confectioners. To tackle its competitors, the Cadbury company had to invest in the latest machinery. In 1866, with a brand-new cocoa press bought from Holland, the company began to produce Cocoa Essence, the very first pure cocoa in the UK. Cadbury also started making the Fancy Box, full of luxury eating chocolates for wealthy customers.

▼ *This late 19th-century advert makes the point that Cadbury's cocoa is 'absolutely pure' – like the pure white cat.*

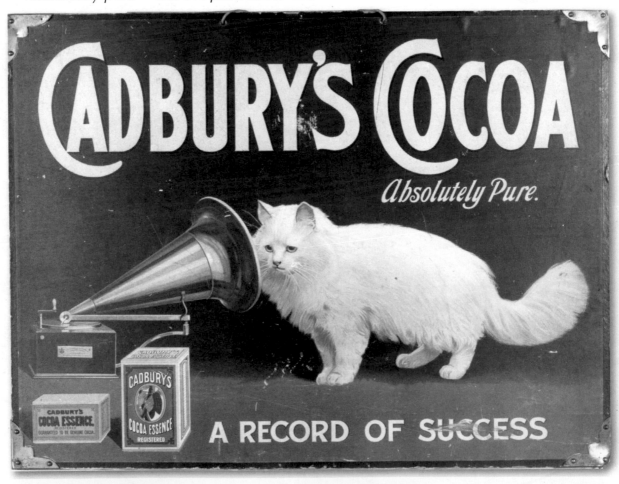

The Cadbury Brothers developed a clever marketing strategy to promote the purity of their new cocoa product with the slogan, 'absolutely pure, therefore best'. The pair employed salesmen to visit doctors in London with samples of Cocoa Essence, and then received letters from medical organizations stating that it was good for people's health. At a time of great concern about unhealthy additives (added ingredients) in food, this support boosted the business greatly.

Brains Behind The Brand

George Cadbury – research and development

George Cadbury had noted that the Dutch manufacturer van Houten had reduced the cocoa fat in its produce from more than 50 to only 30 per cent. This made it possible not to use additives, resulting in a drink that tasted more like chocolate rather than potato flour. George was so keen to discover van Houten's secret that he travelled to Holland to visit the van Houten company. Finding that it had a special de-fatting cocoa press, George persuaded the company to sell him a machine. The way was open to make high-quality cocoa in the UK.

THE COMING OF THE FANCY BOX.

The idea that chocolate boxes should bear pictures instead of printed labels was conceived by Richard Cadbury in 1868. His artistic talent was always invaluable to the business, and it was he who designed the first fancy boxes introduced, as well as numerous box-labels and advertisements. The picture box readily caught the public fancy, and did much to popularise the firm's lines generally. The designs shown are reproduced as a record of his talent as they appear on a page in the "Cadbury Family Book."

▲ *Richard Cadbury illustrated the covers of the Fancy Box himself. The top centre painting shows his six-year-old daughter Jessie with a kitten.*

 It would have been far easier to start a new business, than to pull up a decayed one which had a bad name. The prospect seemed a hopeless one, but we were young and full of energy.

George Cadbury, looking back later in life

Philanthropy: a helping hand

The Quakers were devoted to social reform. They believed businesses should look after their workers and use the profits for the good of the community. The Cadburys treated their workforce well. Workers who arrived punctually for work were treated to breakfast. While they ate, George would read to them and lead discussions to help improve their education. George and Richard Cadbury were among the first Birmingham employers to introduce half days on Saturdays and bank holidays, and they even took the staff on outings.

In 1879 the Cadburys moved the business to a new site called Bournville, 6 kilometres (4 miles) south of Birmingham. Here they built a modern factory with new machinery. From 1894, George Cadbury worked with architect W. Alexander Harvey to construct Bournville village, which provided affordable, good-quality housing for factory workers. Away from the city slums, the village benefited from green fields and open space. In 1900 George gave up his ownership of the estate and set up a charitable trust, Bournville Village Trust, to manage the

▼ *The staff at Bournville prepare for a swimming lesson, around 1910.*

village. Other manufacturers established similar projects, such as Saltaire near Bradford, Yorkshire and Port Sunlight near Liverpool. The Cadbury company's philanthropy continued in the 20th century. For example, in the 1950s, the Schools Department made films, books and project materials for teachers in schools and colleges to help with their lessons. Community investment in the 1990s included Strollerthons – annual 16-kilometre (10-mile) walks to raise money for charity.

▼ *George and Elizabeth Cadbury in 1913.*

Brains Behind The Brand

Elizabeth Cadbury – philanthropist
Unusually for their time, 19th-century Quakers believed that women should have opportunities to gain positions of responsibility. George's wife Elizabeth became known for her charitable work. She was accepted to study at Cambridge University, but opted instead to carry out social work and teach at the Sunday school of her Quaker group. After her marriage, she played an important role in the development of the Bournville Village Trust, and took over as Chairman when George died in 1922. In 1908 she built The Beeches near Bournville, a holiday centre where children from the Birmingham slums could enjoy healthy breaks in the countryside.

" Why it is the very job of life among the villagers! The men not being overworked in the factory go straight to their gardens with keen delight.'
She saw: 'There were gloriously happy youngsters . . . skipping after their fathers . . . with spade and barrow to work their allotments after factory hours. **"**

Annie Diggs, reporter for Cosmopolitan in New York, remarks on the gardens in Bournville village, 1903

Enter Dairy Milk 1900–20

At the start of the new century, the next generation of Cadburys took over the business: Richard's sons Barrow and William alongside George's sons Edward and George. Cocoa was now in great demand. Yet competition in the growing market was on the rise, especially from Dutch and Swiss companies. Fortunately, Cadbury had a novel product.

George Cadbury Junior believed that the key to success was the discovery of a smooth milk chocolate to rival the Swiss products. He finally hit upon a winning recipe, creating Dairy Milk in 1905 – the basic recipe remains similar today. By 1914 it was Cadbury's bestseller. In 1908 a dark chocolate variety, Bournville, was introduced, and it also became an all-time favourite.

Public interest in the the Cadbury chocolate company was growing. In 1902 Cadbury set up a Visitors' Department to run tours around the factory and Bournville village. The tours became extremely popular with members of the public.

▼ *Cadbury products on display in a shop front in the early 1900s.*

Workers in Trinidad in the Caribbean extract cocoa beans from pods, early 1900s.

> Dairy Maid? I wonder you don't call it Dairy Milk, it's a much daintier name.

Cadbury's new milk chocolate bar was to be called Dairy Maid. A salesman told a shopkeeper's daughter about the new product, and her suggestion (above) was accepted.

Owing to the rising demand for chocolate and chocolate products, Cadbury now sought new sources of cocoa beans. Many African and Asian countries, and Pacific islands, started to produce cocoa for the European market.

However, during World War I, Cadbury was forced to cut production because of shortages of sugar and milk. In the final weeks of the war, the company merged with Fry to form the British Cocoa and Chocolate Company (BCCC). Cadbury had the controlling interest (more power) because its assets (items owned by the company, such as buildings and equipment) were three times as great. Together, the two businesses would be stronger to face the challenges ahead.

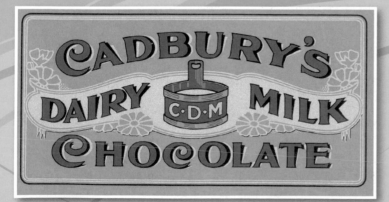

A Cadbury's Dairy Milk wrapper from 1905.

Brains Behind The Brand

Ethics in business

In the early years of the 20th century, evidence surfaced that cocoa from São Tomé and Príncipe (islands off the West African coast ruled by Portugal) was produced by slave labour on its cocoa plantations. Slaves were being brought from Angola. However, Cadbury did not want to stop buying cocoa from the islands, because it would have lost its influence over them. Rather, the company wanted persuade the Portuguese to stop slavery, with the help of the British government. Some people opposed this and accused the Cadburys of profiting from slavery. But US chocolate manufacturers also put pressure on Portugal. Finally, in 1909, Portugal halted the transport of slaves to São Tomé and Príncipe.

After World War I, Cadbury was doing better than competitors Nestlé in Switzerland and Rowntree in York. Dairy Milk continued to be a winner. The 1928 advert, 'a glass and a half of full-cream milk in every half-pound', cleverly used the goodness of milk as a selling point.

To stay ahead, the company continually updated its technology. In 1920, the BCCC began to build Somerdale, a modern factory outside Bristol for Fry. During the 1920s Cadbury modernized the factory at Bournville too. All the processes of producing chocolate were fully automated (done by machine), from pouring in the sugar and cocoa to wrapping the finished products.

In the early 1930s, a major new competitor arose: the US company Mars. It enjoyed extraordinary success with a new range of countlines (see page 15). Mars bars, introduced in 1932, became the best-loved snack. The company also introduced Milky Way in 1935, followed by Maltesers in 1936. Nestlé products were also becoming more popular: in the 1930s, Nestlé's block chocolate was sold in grocers' shops throughout the UK.

Competition with other Quaker companies grew too, especially Rowntree. The old Quaker ties were less important now, and the businesses competed fiercely. Rowntree entered the countline fray with Chocolate Crisp in 1935

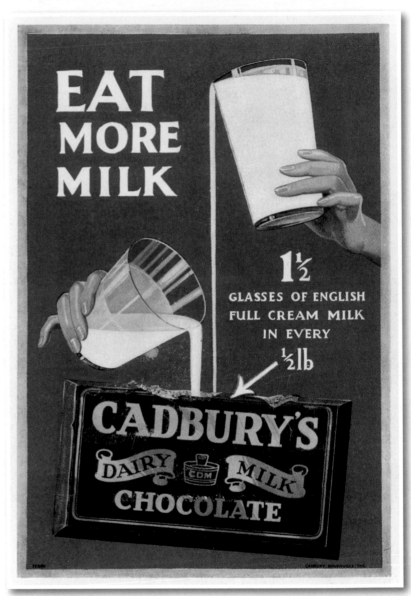

▲ *The famous 'glass and a half of full-cream milk' advert.*

– a wafer covered in chocolate. This simple treat gained immediate popularity; it was soon given the punchier name Kit Kat. Rowntree also introduced the light, bubbly Aero and in 1937, little chocolate beans covered in brightly coloured chocolate, sold in a cardboard tube. Smarties had arrived!

These bar charts show that as the price of Dairy Milk dropped, sales rose sharply.

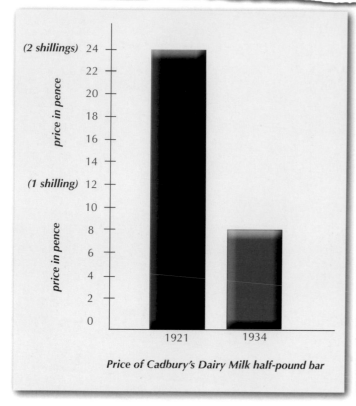

Price of Cadbury's Dairy Milk half-pound bar

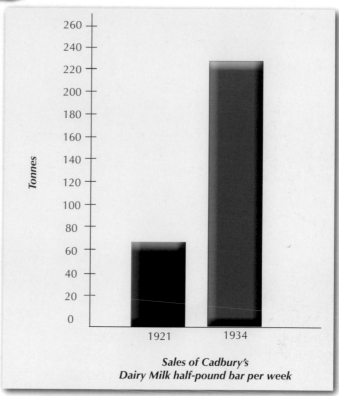

Sales of Cadbury's Dairy Milk half-pound bar per week

Despite the competition, there was space in the market for confectionery companies to grow simply because more people were buying chocolate. By the late 1930s, chocolate was no longer an expensive luxury for many Europeans and Americans. At this time, 1 million Dairy Milk bars and 2 million Chocolate Assortments rolled off the assembly lines every day.

" 101 machines that pounded and churned and cooled and weighed and packed the chocolate, that covered the various bits of confectionery with chocolate, that printed labels and wrappers and cut them up and stuck them on and then packed everything into boxes that some other machine had made. "

Novelist J. B. Priestley describes automation at the Bournville works in 1933

Business Matters

Countlines — A countline is a mixture of cheap ingredients, such as biscuit and wafer, coated with chocolate. This makes countlines far more profitable than solid chocolate. They are called countlines because they are sold by 'count' — quantity — rather than weight.

Business booms 1945–69

During World War II, UK factories were diverted to making weapons and equipment for the war effort, and chocolate production was disrupted. After the war, Cadbury expanded its range to keep ahead of the competition and boosted its advertising.

A popular new addition to the range in 1948 was Fudge, a little snack that became an all-time favourite. A catchy advert, based on the tune from a traditional English folk song, said 'A finger of fudge is just enough to give your kids a treat.' Other new countlines included the Aztec and Picnic bars. A new factory was built specially to produce chocolate biscuits.

After the difficult war years, people had money to spend. The advent of TV in the 1950s brought opportunities for promoting products. Owing to stiff competition, chocolate manufacturers became some of the biggest TV advertisers.

In the UK, Cadbury's advertisement for drinking chocolate was one of the 24 commercials shown on ITV's launch night in 1955. The company focused on making memorable TV adverts with clever one-liners.

In the early 1960s, it introduced a James Bond-style action hero doing dare-devil stunts to deliver chocolates to a beautiful woman: 'All because the lady loves Milk Tray'. Later in the decade, Flake adverts took a sexy approach, showing a beautiful woman losing herself in a moment of chocolate indulgence. Cadbury was doing all it could to stand out from the crowd.

▼ *A Milk Tray advert with a James Bond-style character, 1989.*

An advert for Cadbury's Roses, a variety box of chocolates, which were introduced in 1938. Roses remain popular today.

Brains Behind The Brand

Paul Cadbury – chairman

In 1959, when Paul became chairman, Cadbury was still a family company. The shareholders (people who owned shares in the company) were Fry and Cadbury family members. But because no family members were wealthy enough to buy out other people, none of them could sell their shares to release their capital (get access to their money). More than 50 per cent of shares were owned by the charitable trusts anyway.

In 1962, Paul Cadbury turned the British Cocoa and Chocolate Company into a public company. People could now buy and sell shares in Cadbury. BCCC was no longer owned by the Cadbury and Fry families but by the shareholders, who had no personal interest in the venture but wanted it to be highly profitable.

Business Matters

Retail outlets – A company selling low-priced products needs to get those products into as many shops and outlets as possible to maximize sales. Since chocolate is usually an impulse buy, it is best to position the bars where people are most likely to notice them, for example, next to shop tills.

Cadbury products are sold in:
- Shops, supermarkets, garages
- Vending machines in restaurants, cafés and train stations
- Cinemas, theatres, theme parks
- Transport: buffet cars, aircraft, motorway service stations.

A Cadbury world

Cadbury keeps awareness of its brands high so that they are foremost in the customers' minds when they choose their chocolate. Cadbury carries out promotional work, and marketing campaigns that focus on the taste of the products. It also creates distinctive packaging.

▲ Visitors to one of the Cadbury Tours held at Cadbury World, New Zealand.

Promotional work has long been an important way of raising the company's profile. It began back in 1901, when the Visitors' Department was set up (see page 12). In the 1950s, Cadbury gave out samples and organized cookery demonstrations. The company opened Chocolate Houses – like coffee bars but selling chocolate.

In 1990, Cadbury World opened in Bournville to replace factory tours because they had become so popular that it was no longer practical to admit so many visitors. The visitor attraction built next to the factory, attracted 350,000 visitors in the first year and became one of the UK's favourite tourist locations in the UK. Cadbury World was also set up at the factory in Dunedin, New Zealand in 2003.

From the 1990s, marketing campaigns emphasized the unique Cadbury's taste in the 'Chocolate is Cadbury' campaign. The message was that no other chocolate compares with the Cadbury taste. Advertising also retained elements of the older message about the goodness of the milk in Cadbury's chocolate.

Packaging has always played a significant role in marketing Cadbury products. When customers see a Cadbury product, they instantly recognize it because of key elements: the colour purple, the 'glass and a half' image, the Cadbury script and the packaging design. These give the product a strong brand identity and mark it out from its competitors. The brand is more than just the physical product – it is a combination of the emotional associations that are built up in consumers' minds over time.

The key to creating a successful brand identity is to give each product its own unique look but also to make it clear that it belongs to the Cadbury family, so that customers will immediately link it with Cadbury. Another element is updating the packaging to fit with current tastes – for example, using bright, bold colours – but retaining the link to traditional features by including the original Cadbury script. This makes the product attractive to customers new and old.

Business Matters

Logos – Until 1985, the Cadbury logo varied. It appeared in different colours and was sometimes too small for customers to notice. From 1985, it was decided that a consistent logo should be developed for all Cadbury products. By 2003, complete consistency on all packaging was achieved. This made the branding of products more visible to customers.

▼ *A giant billboard with the glass and a half image – the basic logo has stayed the same since 1928. Compare it with the advert on page 14.*

Cadbury Schweppes 1969–89

Cadbury was a British company that owned a few businesses around the world. In 1969, it merged with the global soft-drinks giant Schweppes in order to become a truly international company. During the 1970s Cadbury Schweppes experienced a big increase in sales.

Cadbury grew its business in new countries, where it had to adapt to the local conditions. For example, in India, a big problem was heat – chocolate on the shop shelves melted! Cadbury had to alter its recipes to produce chocolate that didn't melt quickly. Special countlines were developed that were less sensitive to high temperatures, such as toffee-covered chocolates called Eclairs. Soon, Cadbury India was exporting these new products to other hot countries, including Singapore, Sri Lanka, Hong Kong. These products were often well-received in other countries, too.

In general, Cadbury's expansion in sales was driven by the success of its advertising. It continued to promote its top brands, including Flake, Dairy Milk, Whole Nut, and Fruit and Nut bars. In the 1980s, new products were introduced to great fanfare, such as Wispa and Boost. Wispa, which was introduced with an advertising campaign, 'Have your heard the Wispa?' became one of the most popular bars of the decade.

Cadbury Schweppes also expanded its market share by buying up other confectionery brands.

▼ *India has a huge dairy industry, and Cadbury is a major manufacturer of dairy products there.*

Dominic Cadbury, photographed in 1994, displays a milk chocolate selection. You can see Schweppes products in the background.

Brains Behind The Brand

Dominic Cadbury – Managing Director and Chief Executive
Dominic Cadbury held senior management positions in Cadbury from 1975–2000. Under his leadership, a revolution in production began, the most significant since the Bournville factory was modernized in the 1920s. During the 1980s, the company invested in state-of-the-art chocolate production technology to replace the old production lines. Dominic also streamlined the company's production to focus on the most successful lines, reducing the number of brands produced from 78 to 33.

It purchased several other companies. In 1988 Cadbury Schweppes bought the Lion Confectionery Company, which made fruit gums and pastilles, and in 1989 it purchased Bassett's (which was famous for its liquorice) and Trebor, makers of mints.

Meanwhile, the giant international food companies had their eyes on British chocolate manufacturers, with their well-established brands. In 1988 Rowntree was taken over by Nestlé. Yet Cadbury survived as an independent business – for the time being.

> We had great opportunity, which was that of broadening the market for Cadbury brands geographically . . . That required the concentration of effort behind major brands, the ability to give better value to the customer and more in the way of financial resources than the Firm then possessed.

Adrian Cadbury, the Chairman of Cadbury, explains why it was a good idea to merge with Schweppes in 1969

New markets, new products 1990–2010

Following the collapse of the Communist Soviet Union and Eastern European states in 1989–91, chocolate companies, like other Western businesses, spotted new opportunities. Mars and Cadbury both built factories in Russia; they set up in China too, even though it remained under Communist rule. Cadbury continued to bring out new brands and embraced digital media to promote its products.

Cadbury acquired further businesses, now focusing on drinks companies such as Dr Pepper, 7 Up and Snapple. By now, Cadbury Schweppes was a genuine global international company. In 2008, it demerged into two separate companies again: Cadbury was to focus on chocolate and confectionery, while Schweppes's main concern would be the drinks industry in the USA.

New products were continually developed. In 1996 Fuse launched, and 40 million bars were sold in the first week. Within eight weeks, the snack had become the UK's favourite confectionery! (However, its success proved short-lived; Fuse disappeared from the shelves in 2006.) In 1999 Cadbury launched Miniature Heroes, a tub of miniature bars. Another bright idea was Creme Egg Twisted (launched in 2008) – a bar filled with creme-egg 'goo' to eat all year round not just at Easter.

To boost its brands both new and old at the start of the 21st century, Cadbury aimed to move away from traditional advertising to producing entertaining pieces with broad appeal. A 2007 TV advert for Dairy Milk with a gorilla playing drums to a Phil Collins song became an instant hit in the UK and was soon aired in other countries such as New Zealand and Australia.

An image from the 2012 Goo Games marketing campaign, a games competition with Creme Egg prizes.

The popular 2007 Dairy Milk advert with the drum-playing gorilla. The advert was also displayed on billboards and newspapers.

It was uploaded to YouTube shortly after it was first broadcast. Cadbury reported that sales of Dairy Milk rose by 9 per cent during the campaign.

Digital advertising has become increasingly important because media audiences have become fragmented between a variety of TV channels, the Internet and mobiles. It can give companies wide reach. Cadbury's online Eyebrows advert (2009), in which two schoolchildren's eyebrows dance to a sound track, was a viral marketing winner –

spread by consumers themselves. It achieved four million YouTube viewings in three weeks.

The interactivity of the Internet brings distinct advantages to businesses, allowing people to post comments, enter competitions and vote. Customers can offer opinions about the company's products, and the company can respond. This interaction with consumers is the 21st-century version of the cookery demonstrations and promotions of the 1950s.

Business Matters

Product development — Cadbury has a loyal following for its brands but always has to think about developing new products too. There is a defined process for this. See the chart below.

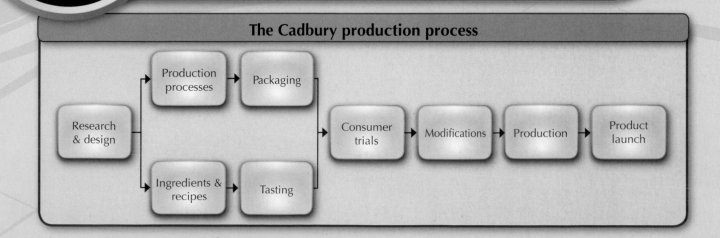

The Cadbury production process

Research & design → Production processes → Packaging

Research & design → Ingredients & recipes → Tasting

→ Consumer trials → Modifications → Production → Product launch

Purple Goes Green

At the start of the new millennium, Cadbury established programmes to help the environment, aiming to reduce its use of energy, packaging and water. The company launched Purple Goes Green in 2007 and made moves towards fair trade.

In an attempt to reduce carbon emissions, the company examined its transport needs. From 2003, Cadbury streamlined its distribution to reduce 'food miles' – the distance a food travels from where it's produced to where it's sold. Instead of 63 haulage (transport) suppliers, Cadbury gave the haulage and distribution work to just five suppliers, which made transporting its goods more efficient. Cadbury also worked to reduce 'empty running' – when a lorry delivers goods and returns empty to the depot – to under 25 per cent. These types of measures are good for the environment and keep down costs too.

▼ *Farm workers in Ghana sorting through cocoa beans that have been spread out to dry in the sun.*

Innovations have reduced energy use in warehouses. At two sites, heat-sensitive lights ensure that electricity is not wasted when no one is there. Cadbury's Milton Keynes warehouse runs on 'green electricity', from renewable sources such as wind power. The warehouse at Minworth, West Midlands is Europe's largest chilled warehouse, but the chillers are not on all the time. They run only at night, when energy is cheaper; this cuts bills by 40 per cent.

The Cadbury Cocoa Partnership, a 10-year plan introduced in 2008, is another eco scheme. The company invests in cocoa farms in Ghana, India, Indonesia and the Caribbean. It aims to help farmers to increase their cocoa yields and start new rural businesses. The scheme improves their lives by supporting education, the environment and the building of wells.

As part of the Cadbury Cocoa Partnership, from 2009 Cadbury's Dairy Milk used only Fairtrade cocoa. The amount of Fairtrade cocoa sourced from Ghana immediately tripled. Under the scheme, Cadbury agreed to pay a guaranteed minimum price for cocoa, even if the price on the world market fell below it.

Brains Behind The Brand

Brains behind the brand – Todd Stitzer, Chief Strategy Officer 2000-2010

Todd Stitzer believed that the old Quaker values could still apply to the Cadbury businesses. They could make profits for shareholders and help society too. In 2006 he set a target of 1 per cent of pre-tax profits to go to programmes to benefit communities where Cadbury operated. This target was always beaten.

> " In Ghana there is a phrase 'Kookoo cotanpa', which means 'Cocoa is a good parent; it looks after you.' We hope with this initiative Cadbury and our partners can be a good parent to cocoa. "
>
> *James Boateng, Managing Director of Cadbury Ghana*

The end of an era

By 2000, Cadbury was the only independent survivor of England's Quaker chocolate families. Rowntree, Terry and Fry had all been taken over. Cadbury was also the world's largest confectionery company.

Yet Cadbury was changing. In 2000, Dominic Cadbury stepped down as chairman. For the first time, no family member sat on the Cadbury board. By this time, fewer than 1 per cent of shares were in family hands. Cadbury's shareholders were investors with no personal links to the business.

In 2009, Irene Rosenfeld, the chair of the international US-based food company Kraft arranged to meet the Cadbury chairman, Roger Carr. She said: 'You know, I have this great idea that we should buy you.' Roger Carr was not keen to sell, but in the end, he did. How did this happen?

▼ *Cadbury workers protest in London in 2010, fearing job losses when Kraft took over the company.*

The prospect of a takeover of Cadbury sent shares soaring. Many short-term investors, such as hedge funds, hoped for a quick profit by buying shares and then selling them once the price had risen. By January 2010, short-term investors owned 31 per cent of Cadbury.

Carr realized the business would be sold, so he pushed Rosenfeld to offer a higher price per share, so that the shareholders would make more money. Kraft then offered another 20p per share. Rosenfeld took her offer straight to the shareholders, and they voted 'yes' to Kraft taking over Cadbury. In 2010 Kraft bought Cadbury at a cost of £11.5 billion (US $18 billion) – one of the biggest business deals in British history. Afterwards, Roger Carr commented: 'I fought for the shareholders. I'm paid by the shareholders and I delivered huge value for the shareholders with the board – that is my responsibility.'

Many British people were against the takeover, and some refused to buy Kraft products. Even the British government protested when Kraft announced the closure of the Somerdale factory, with the loss of 400 jobs. Then in December 2011, Kraft planned to cut a further 200 jobs at Cadbury in the UK. Despite these job losses, Kraft insisted that it would continue to invest in Cadbury and ensure the success of this historic and world-famous chocolate company for years to come.

> " It is hard to ignore the fact that the fate of a company with a long history and many tens of thousands of employees was decided by people who had not owned the company a few weeks earlier and had no intention of owning it a few weeks later. "
>
> **Peter Mandelson, British Secretary of State for Business, March 2010**

Cadbury's chocolate remained popular ➤ after the takeover by Kraft. In 2012, Cadbury was the official treat provider to the London Olympic Games.

To create a new product, it is helpful to put together a product development brief like the one below. This is a sample brief for Chocolate Bars.

The SWOT analysis on the page opposite can help you to think about the strengths and weaknesses of your products, and the opportunities and threats presented. This helps you to see how practical your idea is before you consider investing in it.

Product Development Brief

Name of application: Chocolate Bars

Type of product: Café

The product explained (use 25 words or less): Reviving an earlier tradition of Chocolate Houses from the 1950s, Chocolate Bars will serve a range of chocolate-based drinks, including healthy low-fat and low-sugar options.

Target age of users: All ages. An ideal place to socialize for families, young people and the elderly.

What will the bars provide? A wide range of non-alcoholic chocolate-based drinks and snacks, serving alternatives to alcoholic and caffeine-based beverages. They will be open all day and in the evenings, providing an alternative venue to pubs.

Are there any similar products available? There are some independent chocolate houses but none run by a major chocolate brand like Cadbury.

What makes your venture different? There are many bars and cafés but few cafés that focus on chocolate products. Chocolate is a hugely popular, inexpensive treat, so the Chocolate Bars have potential.

Name of Cadbury venture you are assessing . . . Chocolate Bars. The information below will help you assess the venture. By addressing all four areas, you can make your venture stronger and more likely to be a success.

Questions to consider	*Strengths*
Is your venture unique?	*It is unusual in the global marketplace.*
Is there anything innovative about it?	*The idea has been tried before, in the 1950s, but is innovative in the current market.*
What are its USPs? (unique selling points)	*Caffeine- and alcohol-free refreshments from Fairtrade sources. Open in the evenings.*
Why will people go to a Chocolate Bar rather than a regular café?	*Appeal to people who do not tend to go to pubs, such as young people and the elderly.*

	Weaknesses
Why wouldn't people go to a Chocolate Bar?	*May think the refreshments are unhealthy.*
Does it live up to the claims you make?	*Low-caffeine, low-sugar products, but in general, chocolate-based drinks and snacks are less healthy than some alternatives.*
Is it as good or better than other types of café?	*Although focused on chocolate products, in other ways would be similar to other cafes.*
Are the potential losses worth risking the heavy investment needed to start up the Chocolate Bars?	*High-risk venture due to cost of obtaining, refitting and running Bars before making a profit.*

	Opportunities
Could the range of products offered expand in the future?	*Yes. If successful, the Bars could offer a wider range of chocolate-based products.*
Could they be established globally?	*Yes. They would have great appeal in Muslim countries where alcohol is not consumed.*

	Threats
Will the Chocolate Bars face too much competition from other cafés?	*There may be no market for new cafés.*
Are any of the weaknesses so bad that they might affect the success of the venture in the long term?	*There are no obvious weaknesses that would affect the long-term success of the venture.*

Do you have what it takes to work at Cadbury? Try this!

Cadbury employs people in a wide range of jobs, including customer service, logistics, management, manufacturing, marketing, research and development.

1. You're eating a bar of chocolate. What are your thoughts?
a) This snack is delicious! Wish I had two.
b) This is tasty but a bit too sweet.
c) This bar would be even tastier if the texture could be a little lighter and smoother, and perhaps a new fruity flavour would be good.

2. You unwrap a confectionery gift and …
a) Enjoy it quickly before anyone else asks to share.
b) Wonder why it takes so long to unwrap – there seems to be a lot of packaging.
c) Realizing there is a lot of packaging, you dream up a great idea for lighter packaging that would work just as well.

3. You're working on a school project with a group of mates, but one of them isn't pulling her weight. What do you do?
a) Ignore her and get on with the project.
b) Do the work yourself so as not to hold up the others.
c) Have a chat with the whole team about sharing the workload. If anyone is finding it hard, the others can help out.

4. You're supposed to be going out with a group of friends to celebrate the end of term but no one has decided where to go. Do you:
a) Complain to your mates.
b) Ask people where they'd like to go.
c) Come up with two possible ideas and ask people to choose which they'd prefer and get back to you within three days.

5. To raise awareness of local voluntary work, the school has organized a volunteering day in the community. What do you do?
a) Try to pick the project that will involve the least effort.
b) Ask if you can work at your favourite project.
c) Ask if you can organize one of the groups. This is a great opportunity to develop your teamwork skills.

6. You realize that several parents are driving children to a sports club, while others have a long journey on two buses. What do you do?
a) Nothing – it's not your problem.
b) Offer a friend a lift with you to the club.
c) Talk to all the families involved and arrange lift-sharing to save fuel and money.

Results

Mostly As: You don't seem to be thinking about how to build up skills for your future career. Why not think about your strengths and see if you could develop them through schoolwork or community projects?

Mostly Bs: You're clearly keen to learn and have ideas that would be useful to a potential employer. See if you can develop these further through schoolwork or community projects.

Mostly Cs: It sounds like you already have some skills that would be valuable to a company like Cadbury. Keep working on them through schoolwork or community projects and maybe one day you'll work for a chocolate company!

Glossary

brand   A kind of product made by a particular company under a particular name. For example, Dairy Milk is a brand made by Cadbury.

capital   Wealth, perhaps in the form of money or shares in a company, that a person owns.

charitable trust   An organization run by a group of people called trustees, who manage the organization for a charity.

cocoa   A powder made from roasted and ground cocoa beans, mixed with hot milk or water to make a hot drink.

countline   A snack partly made from chocolate but includes other ingredients such as biscuit.

discrimination   Treating people unfairly, for example because of their sex or race.

drinking chocolate   A mixture of cocoa powder, milk solids and sugar, added to hot milk or water to make a chocolate drink.

Fairtrade   Trade between companies in wealthy countries and traders in poor countries in which fair prices are paid to the producers.

franchise   When a company allows another company to carry out a particular activity or service for it. For example, Cadbury used to give franchises to other companies to make Cadbury chocolate.

hedge fund   A group of investors who take high risks to invest money in order to try to make a big profit.

innovation   A new method, idea or product.

logo   A symbol adopted by an organization to identify its products.

marketing   Promoting and selling goods or services, including advertising and market research (finding out what people want).

merge   When two or more companies combine to form a single company.

multinational company   A company that operates in several countries.

pestle and mortar   A pestle is a heavy tool with a rounded end, used for crushing foods, usually in a cup-shaped container called a mortar.

pre-tax profits   The profits that a company makes before it pays tax.

promotional work   Creating publicity about a product so that large numbers of people find out about it.

public company   A company that members of the public can invest in.

Quaker   A member of the Society of Friends, a Christian religious group that is strongly opposed to violence and war.

shareholder   An owner of shares in a company.

short-term investor   Someone who invests money in the hope of making a profit quickly.

slum   District where poor people live, with bad housing and living conditions.

streamline   To adopt faster or simpler working methods so that products can be made more quickly and easily.

subsidiary company   A company that is controlled by another company because the other company owns the majority of the shares in it.

takeover   When one company buys out another one, and takes control of it.

viral marketing   A form of marketing in which people pass on information about a company's goods to each other on the Internet.

Index

BIG BU$INE$$

Contents of all the titles in the series:

Apple
978 0 7502 7090 8

An Apple in every home
The origins of Apple
Building the Apple brand
Fallout at the top
Steve returns to Apple
Riding the Internet wave
Apple explores music
The invention of the iPhone
There's an app for that!
Apple takes on publishing
What makes Apple so 'must-have'?
What does the future hold for Apple?
Design your own App for the App Store!
Do you have what it takes to work at Apple?

Disney
978 0 7502 6922 3

Disney on top
The birth of Mickey Mouse
Snow White and the Seven Oscars
Disney in your living room
The birth of the theme park
Life and death at Disney
The wonderful world of Disney
Disney grows up
A store in every town
Disney Interactive
Steadying the ship
What does the future hold for Disney?
Design your own Disney venture
Do you have what it takes to work at Disney?

Microsoft
978 0 7502 6924 7

Riding high
From small beginnings
The launch of MS-DOS
Opening Windows, 1983
'A computer on every desk'
Bill Gates: the man behind Microsoft
The Internet takes off
New Windows to the world
Entering the games world: Xbox
Into the clouds
Microsoft in the community
Microsoft's vision
Develop your own Microsoft product
Do you have what it takes to work at Microsoft?

Cadbury
978 0 7502 6923 0

Sweet success
The founder: John Cadbury
Building the business 1861-1900
Philanthropy: a helping hand
Enter Dairy Milk 1900-20
Facing the competition 1920-45
Business booms 1945-69
A Cadbury world
Cadbury Schweppes 1969-89
New markets, new products 1990-2010
Purple goes green
The end of an era
Design your own Cadbury venture
Do you have what it takes to work at Cadbury?

Facebook
978 0 7502 7088 5

Birth of a new brand
Facebook Inc
The site at a glance
The idea keeps on growing
An expert on board
Making popularity pay
To high school and beyond
Going global
The secret to making money
There's more to Facebook than friends
To share or not to share?
What's next for Facebook?
Invent your own Facebook app
Do you have what it takes to work at Facebook?

Nike
978 0 7502 6925 4

Nike rules the world
The birth of the business
Growing the company
Better by design
The Nike brand is born
First hiccups
Built on innovation
Star power
Life at Nike HQ
Coming through adversity
Going global
What does the future hold for Nike?
Do you have what it takes to work at Nike?

Coca-Cola
978 0 7502 6921 6

Coca-Cola at the top
'A delicious and refreshing beverage'
Coke and the American way of life
New-look Coke - the 'real thing'
Coke and sports
New markets, new drinks
Coca-Cola controversies
Coca-Cola: a marketing miracle
The challenge of sustainability
Corporate social responsibility (CSR)
Muhtar Kent, head of Coca-Cola
'2020 Vision': Coca-Cola's future
Design your own Coca-Cola venture
Do you have what it takes to work at Coca Cola?

Google
978 0 7502 7089 2

The world gets Googled!
What makes Google so good?
Google is born
Setting up the company
Standing out from the competition
Making a profit
Keeping the staff happy
Google goes public
Expanding the business
Diversifying the business
Google changes the world
Making Google future-proof
Invent the next Google product!
Do you have what it takes to work at Google?

Nintendo
978 0 7502 7091 5

Nintendo rules the world!
Seizing the opportunity
From playing cards to electronics
Building a reputation for fun
The Game Boy arrives!
The battle for your living room
The business of games creation
Expanding the games market
Mario – the superstar for 30 years!
Games the whole family can play
Games for everyday life
Making plans for the future
Invent a new Nintendo game!
Do you have what it takes to work at Nintendo?

WAYLAND